DATE DUE | BORROWER'S NAME | NO.

W9-CBL-091

POISONOUS LIZARDS

Gila Monsters and Mexican Beaded Lizards

by James Martin

Illustrated with photographs
by Joe McDonald

Reading consultant:

John Manning, Professor of Reading, University of Minnesota

Capstone Press

Minneapolis

Printed in the United States of America.

Capstone Press • 2440 Fernbrook Lane • Minneapolis, MN 55447

Editorial Director   John Coughlan
Managing Editor   John Martin
Copy Editor   Gil Chandler

Library of Congress Cataloging-in-Publication Data

Martin, James, 1950-
    Poisonous lizards: Gila monsters and Mexican beaded
    lizards / by James Martin
        p. cm.
    Includes bibliographical references and index.
    ISBN 1-56065-240-3
    1. Gila monster--Juvenile literature. 2. Mexican beaded
    lizard--Juvenile literature. [1. Gila monster. 2. Mexican
    beaded lizard.]   I. Title.
    QL666.L247M37   1995
    597'.95--dc20   94-30620
                                                              CIP
                                                              AC

ISBN: 1-56065-240-3

99 98 97 96 95   8 7 6 5 4 3 2 1

Table of Contents

Facts about Gila Monsters and Mexican Beaded Lizards

Scientific name: *Heloderma suspectum* (Gila monster) *and Heloderma horridum* (Mexican beaded lizard)

Description: The Gila monster is the largest lizard in the United States. The Mexican beaded lizard is even larger.

Length: Gila monsters are 14 to 16 inches (36 to 40 centimeters) at maturity. Mexican beaded lizards are as long as 35 inches (90 centimeters).

Weight: Gila monsters are 16 to 24 ounces (0.45 to 0.67 kilograms) at maturity.

Physical features: The skin is composed of beaded scales containing bits of bone.

Color: The Gila monster's skin is black with four bands or other markings in orange, yellow, pink, or red. The Mexican beaded lizard is dark with six white, cream, or yellow bands or other markings.

Distinctive habits: Both lizards spend most of their time hiding in holes or under rocks. They move with an awkward waddle. They are fierce and tireless fighters.

Food: Both Gila monsters and Mexican beaded lizards eat rodents, baby birds, and eggs.

Reproductive cycle: Both lizards mate in spring and lay their eggs 45 days later. Gila monsters lay an average clutch of 3 to 5 eggs. The larger Mexican beaded lizards lay an average

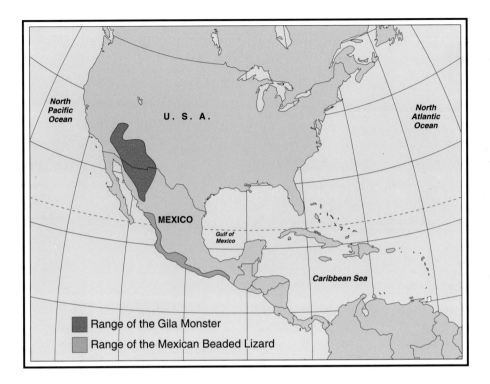

clutch of 10 eggs. After an incubation period of about 10 months, the young hatch the following spring.

Life span: 20 to 30 years in captivity. Their average lifespan in the wild is unknown.

Range: The Gila monster is found in the Colorado Plateau and in the Sonoran and Mojave deserts of the southwestern U.S. and northern Mexico. The Mexican beaded lizard lives in the western coastal areas of Mexico.

Habitat: Gila monsters live in hot, scrubby deserts. The Mexican beaded lizard is found in woodland areas.

Chapter 1

Poisonous Lizards

Under a flat rock in the desert, a lizard seeks the shade. The lizard is covered with orange and black dots. It has a flat head, a stubby tail, and a thick body. Its bright purple mouth and black tongue look strange against its orange skin. A shadow passes over its hiding place. The lizard pulls back. It's frightened– but ready to fight.

This shy creature is the Gila monster, the largest lizard in the United States. Along with the Mexican beaded lizard, it is one of only two poisonous lizards in the world.

Tree roots and flat rocks make a good hiding place for this Gila monster.

The Origins of the Gila Monster

Gila monsters are **descendants** of monitor lizards. The Komodo dragon, the world's largest lizard, is a monitor. Monitors came from **mosasaurs**, huge sea-going lizards that lived in the age of dinosaurs. Mosasaurs grew to 50 feet (15 meters) long.

In the past, close relatives of the Gila monster lived in much of North America. Now they live only in the deserts of the southwest. Nobody knows why they live in such a small area today.

Scientists know little about the life and habits of the Gila monster. They do know that Gila monsters spend most of their lives hiding under rocks. There, they are shaded from the burning sun. They are also safe from **predators**.

A famous dinosaur hunter, Professor Edward Drinker Cope, gave the Gila monster its scientific name, *Heloderma suspectum*. In

The Gila monster crawls out from its hiding place.

8

the Greek language, *helo* means "nail" or "stud," and *derma* means "skin." Cope named the species *suspectum* because he suspected they were poisonous.

The Gila Monster's Size

Gila monsters reach 14 to 16 inches (36 to 40 centimeters) in length and weigh 16 to 24 ounces (0.45 to 0.67 kilograms). In **captivity** they grow larger and heavier. The longest Gila monster reached 21 inches (53 centimeters). The heaviest weighed in at 4.75 pounds (2.1 kilograms).

The Mexican Beaded Lizard

The Mexican beaded lizard is closely related to the Gila monster. It is larger than the Gila monster–up to three feet (1 meter) long. It is slimmer and usually darker, with yellow scales. Its head is completely black, and its tongue is pink.

The beaded lizard has six or seven bands across its tail. Gila monsters have only four bands. The tail makes up less than half the Gila monster's length, but most of the length of the Mexican beaded lizard.

Range

There are two types of Gila monsters. The Arizona Gila monster lives in Arizona. Black patches cover its light skin.

The banded Gila monster roams western Arizona. Most of its skin is orange or pink. It has bands of black around its body.

Both types of Gila monsters may also be found in the state of Sonora, in northern Mexico. A few live in the parts of California, Nevada, Utah, and New Mexico that border Arizona.

The Mexican beaded lizard lives on the dry western coast of Mexico and in Guatemala.

Gila monsters live in the dry areas of the southwest United States and northern Mexico.

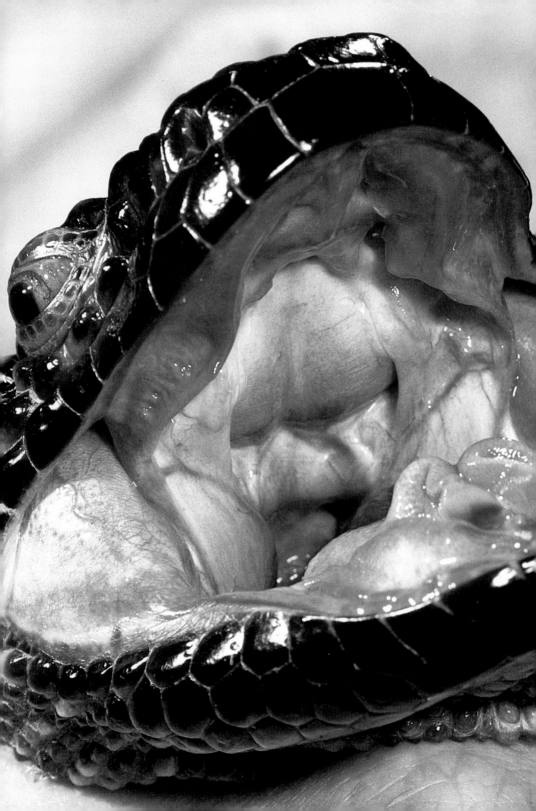

Chapter 2

Teeth, Venom, and Skin

The ancient tyrannosaurs had skulls that looked like huge Gila monster heads. Both animals have large eye sockets and rows of sharp teeth in their jaws.

Gila Monster Teeth

Gila monster teeth are unlike the teeth of any other animal. They do not carve their **prey**, like the teeth of tyrannosaurs or sharks. Instead, they curve back to get a firm grip. When a Gila monster bites down, it grips for

The mouth of the Gila monster is deadly to its victims.

The Gila monster can eat some things, such as eggs, without the use of its venom.

minutes at a time. This allows poison to enter the bloodstream of its victim.

Poisonous snakes have fangs that work differently. They are like doctors' needles. **Venom** travels down a tube inside the tooth to the tip of the fang. When the fang pierces the skin, the snake squeezes its poison gland–which sits in the roof of its mouth–and

16

squirts venom into its victim. The snake can then quickly pull back to safety.

Gila monsters and Mexican beaded lizards dribble their poison along grooves on the outsides of their teeth. Because the poison moves slowly, these lizards must keep biting and not let go. With their strong jaws, they chew the venom into the prey.

A Scientific Mistake

Because Gila monsters don't have fangs, the first scientists to study them thought they couldn't possibly be poisonous. The scientists also couldn't find Gila monsters' venom glands. They decided that **bacteria** in the lizards' mouths must infect bitten animals, causing them to get sick and die.

But the scientists were wrong. The poison glands in a Gila monster lie under the lower teeth, where the scientists didn't think to look.

How Deadly?

There are many stories of people dying from Gila monster bites, but these stories probably

aren't true. The poison does cause terrible pain. The skin around the bite often swells. The blood pressure of the victim may drop. A Gila monster or Mexican beaded lizard bite may also cause **nausea**, dizziness, and other sicknesses. But the pain goes away in a few hours. In a week or two, most victims feel fine. Even a small child can survive the bite of a Gila monster or Mexican beaded lizard.

Gila monsters and Mexican beaded lizards may use their poison to hurt, not kill, their prey.

The World's only Poisonous Lizards

The origin of the venom in Gila monsters and Mexican beaded lizards is a mystery. Of all the earth's lizards, only these two–living in the same small region–are poisonous. Why? And why do lizards have such a slow way of injecting venom, unlike snakes? Scientists are still looking for the answers.

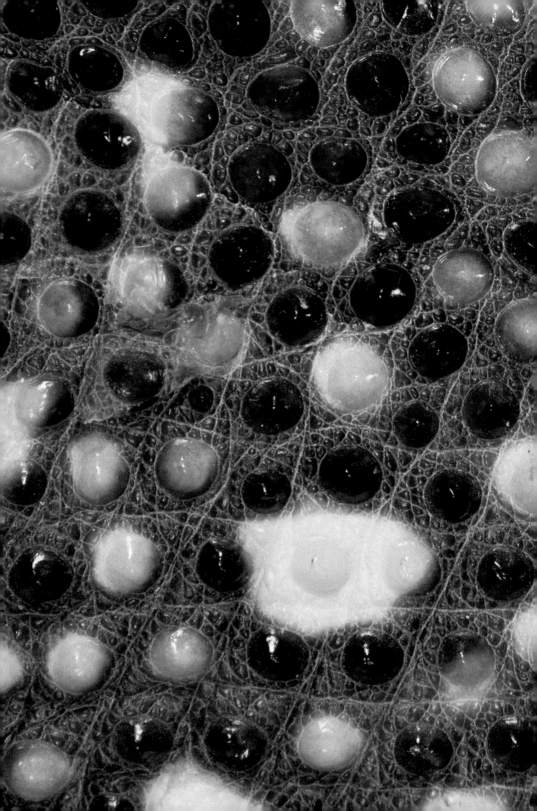

Armor

The armor of Gila monsters and Mexican beaded lizards is beaded skin. Each bead contains a small piece of bone called an **osteoderm**. The osteoderms protect the lizards from the sharp teeth and claws of their enemies. Many dinosaurs had this kind of skin. Komodo dragons also have osteoderms. But only Gila monsters and Mexican beaded lizards have full suits of osteoderm armor.

Camouflage

The color of the Gila monster acts like **camouflage**. This makes it hard to see. To an enemy, the lizard looks like a rock or a shadow.

The scales around the mouth and eyes are always black. This allows the small black eyes of the Gila monster to disappear into its skin.

The skin of the Mexican beaded lizard acts as armor and as camouflage to protect it from enemies.

Chapter 3

Tall Tales about Gila Monsters

Pioneers in the old West loved to exaggerate. For them, tall tales were the best kinds of stories. And Gila monster stories were the best kinds of tall tales.

As late as the middle of this century, some books claimed that a drop of Gila monster saliva would poison an area 20 feet (about six meters) across. Nothing would grow there for ten years, they said. And any animal that crossed the area supposedly would drop dead on the spot.

A Cowboy Story

Stories from the old West describe Gila monsters as indestructible beasts. One cowboy told about his amazing battle with an especially tough Gila.

First, the cowboy hit the lizard with a club. This only made it mad. Then he fired his revolver four times. The bullets just bounced off the Gila monster's tough skin.

The lizard fought back. It grabbed the cowboy's revolver in its jaws and dragged the man toward a river. The cowboy fired a shot down its throat, which blasted the lizard's body in two. The head and front legs jumped into the river and swam away with the cowboy's gun.

An Unreliable Newspaper Report

Old newspapers also told tall tales about Gila monsters. An 1883 edition of the *Arizona Sentinel* reported the capture of a 300-pound (135-kilogram) specimen. Another newspaper challenged the *Sentinel* to prove the story. The *Sentinel* couldn't come up with witnesses or evidence.

The fearsome-looking Gila monster is the subject of many "tall tales."

Chapter 4

Life as a Poisonous Lizard

The truth about Gila monsters and Mexican beaded lizards is as interesting as any tall tale. The ability of these animals to survive difficult conditions is amazing.

Immune to Venom

Gila monsters and Mexican beaded lizards are immune to rattlesnake bites, which are deadly to most desert creatures. They also can survive the venom of other poisonous lizards.

A young Gila monster finishes eating an egg.

Impossible to Drown

The lizards are also nearly impossible to drown. People have tried to kill them by tying them to rocks and keeping them under water. Lizards can live without air for long periods. Even 12 hours underwater may not kill one.

One man put a Gila monster in a full bathtub. He left for a week-long trip, and forgot about the reptile. When he returned, the Gila monster was floating like a cork on the water–still alive and fast asleep.

No other lizard can match the endurance of the Gila monster or the Mexican beaded lizard. Males sometimes fight for hours without stopping to rest.

Temperature

In the summer, temperatures in the desert can rise as high as 120 degrees Fahrenheit (49 degrees Celsius) or higher. The ground becomes even hotter than the air.

Gila monsters seek shelter under rocks and in holes if the temperature reaches 90 degrees Fahrenheit (32 degrees Celsius). Although they live in a hot climate, they can't survive high body temperatures. If they stayed in the sun a long time, they would die.

Unlike other reptiles, Gila monsters seem comfortable when temperatures drop. They move about in 50 degree Fahrenheit (10 degree Celsius) temperatures. At that temperature, most snakes and lizards hide in warm burrows

Burrows

Gila monsters and Mexican beaded lizards sleep in different places in different seasons. In spring and summer, they rest among the desert rocks. To keep cool, they stay under trees or bushes. They usually rest alone, but sometimes up to six Gila monsters will inhabit a single **burrow**.

Hibernation

In the winter, Gila monsters and Mexican beaded lizards stay in safe hiding places. They enter a quiet state that is like **hibernation**.

But their burrows, called **hibernacula**, attract other reptiles. Scientists have found large hibernacula that contain rattlesnakes, tortoises, Gila monsters, and other lizards. Gila monsters and Mexican beaded lizards spend more than half of their lives resting in these hibernacula.

During the spring and summer, they grow fat and find mates. They are most active in May. Even during the active season–about three months each year–they spend nearly all of their time resting underground.

Gila monsters and Mexican beaded lizards use their long claws to climb.

Climbing

Gila monsters and Mexican beaded lizards usually stay on the ground. But they will climb trees, bushes, or cacti to raid bird nests. Steep rocks are no problem, either.

Gila monsters always climb up and down head first. When they climb downward, they use their rear claws to grip the plant. Their front feet inch downward. They move in a slow and clumsy way, but they rarely fall.

Food

Because Gila monsters and Mexican beaded lizards are slow, they like to hunt food that can't move. An egg, for example, is the perfect prey. These lizards will swallow eggs whole. They also break the shells to drink the contents.

Baby birds that can't fly also can become tasty meals. Sometimes rabbits or mice stumble into the jaws of hungry Gila monsters.

Gila monsters can eat up to half their weight at one time. They store extra fat in their tail. The fat nourishes them during their long, sleepy winters.

A Gila monster breaks the shell of a quail egg and licks up its contents.

Chapter 5

Mating and Reproduction

In the spring, after leaving their hibernacula for the season, male Gila monsters will fight one another for the chance to mate. These savage fights may last for hours. The larger lizard almost always wins.

When the winning male meets a female, he nuzzles her chin, licks her skin, and caresses her nose. A month and a half after mating, the female leaves about a dozen eggs in a small, shallow hole.

Venomous Babies

The eggs hatch the following spring. When the babies break out of their shells, they already have sharp teeth and poisonous venom. The baby lizards will bite if someone tries to pick them up or carry them. These bites cause intense pain but are not deadly. Still,

zookeepers are always careful when handling Gila monsters.

Lifespan

In **captivity**, Gila monsters live twenty to thirty years. How long they live in the wild is still a mystery. Some day, scientists will tag and follow wild Gila monsters so that we can discover their natural **lifespans**.

Chapter 6
The Future

Gila monsters and Mexican beaded lizards are the perfect size to be the prey of coyotes, rattlesnakes, and hawks. Their toughness and their venom, however, make them too much trouble to kill.

Human Enemies

People are the only real enemy of Gila monsters and Mexican beaded lizards. People can keep their distance and kill the lizards with

The Mexican beaded lizard

clubs or guns. Most of the lizards, however, are accidentally killed while crossing busy roads.

Human Uses

There are many laws against the export of Gila monsters. But people still capture Gila monsters illegally. They sell the lizards to collectors who pay a lot of money for them.

Some people claim that Gila monster venom can cure diseases. Long ago, people would drink Gila monster venom to cure paralysis. There's no proof that this works. Yet people still hunt the Gila monster for its venom.

Endangered

No one knows for sure if the population of Gila monsters is getting larger or smaller. The population growth of humans, however, is a threat to the lizard's **habitat**. We clear the desert vegetation to build houses. Growing cities also destroy the homes of Gila monsters and Mexican beaded lizards.

   Because people are afraid of Gila monsters,
they may kill them or move them to areas
where they can't survive. Some Gila monsters
live on protected land such as parks and
wilderness areas. These lizards need a lot of
room to find safe nests and food. If we don't
protect enough land, Gila monsters and
Mexican beaded lizards may not survive.

Glossary

bacteria–tiny one-celled organisms

burrow–a hole in which an animal lives

camouflage–a color pattern that helps an animal hide itself by blending into its surroundings

captivity–the state of being captured

descendant–one who is linked to a past species

habitat–the natural surroundings in which an animal lives

hibernacula–resting places used for several months every winter. A single resting place is called a hibernaculum.

hibernation–a quiet state in which an animal rests and stores up energy for more active months

lifespan–the length of an animal's life

mosasaurs–huge, prehistoric, swimming lizards

nausea–a stomach sickness that causes a feeling of the need to vomit

osteoderm–a small piece of bone. Many of these make up the outer skin of a Gila monster.

predator–an animal that hunts other animals for food

prey–an animal that is hunted

venom–the poison used by snakes and lizards to harm their prey

To Learn More

Hiser, Iona Seibert. *The Gila Monster*. Austin, TX: Steck-Vaughn, 1972.

Gravelle, Karen. *Lizards*. New York: F. Watts, 1991.

Harrison, Virginia. *The World of Lizards*. Milwaukee: G. Stevens, 1988

Stidworthy, John. *Reptiles and Amphibians*. New York: Facts on File, 1989.

Lampton, Christopher. *Endangered Species*. New York: F. Watts, 1988.

Fichter, George S. *Poisonous Animals*. New York: F. Watts, 1991.

Arnold, Caroline. *Watching Desert Wildlife*. Minneapolis: Carolrhoda, 1994.

Twist, Clint. *Deserts*. New York: Dillon, 1991.

Wiewandt, Thomas. *The Hidden Life of the Desert*. New York: Crown, 1990.

Some Useful Addresses

Friends of the Earth
218 D St. S.E.
Washington, DC 20003

Friends of the Earth/Les Ami(e)s de la terre
251 Laurier Ave., #701
Ottawa ON K1P 5J6

The Nature Conservancy
1815 N. Lynn Street
Arlington, VA 22209

Society for the Study of Amphibians and Reptiles
P.O. Box 626
Hays, KS 67601-0626

**Canadian Amphibian and
Reptile Conservation Society**
9 Mississauga Rd. N., #1
Mississauga ON L5H

Index